Penguin Books
Open Heart University

Spike Milligan was born at Ahmednagar in India in
1919. He received his first education in a tent in the
Hyderabad Sindh desert and graduated from there
through a series of Roman Catholic schools in
India and England to the Lewisham Polytechnic.
Always something of a playboy, he then plunged
into the world of Show Business, seduced by his
first stage appearance, at the age of eight, in the
nativity play of his Poona convent school. He
began his career as a band musician but has since
become famous as a humorous script writer and
actor in both films and broadcasting. He was one of
the main figures in and behind the infamous Goon
Show. Among the films he has appeared in are:
Suspect, Invasion, Postman's Knock and *Milligan at
Large*. Spike Milligan has also published *The Little
Potboiler, Silly Verse for Kids, Dustbin of Milligan, A
Book of Bits, The Bed-Sitting Room* (a play), *The Bald
Twit Lion, A Book of Milliganimals, Puckoon,
Transports of Delight, Small Dreams of a Scorpion*,
and his war memoirs, *Adolf Hitler: My Part in His
Downfall, 'Rommel?' 'Gunner Who?', Monty: His
Part in My Victory* and *Mussolini: His Part in My
Downfall*. Among his latest publications are *The
Milligan Book of Records, Games, Cartoons and
Commercials; Dip the Puppy; William McGonagall:
The Truth at Last* (with Jack Hobbs); and *The Spike
Milligan Letters*, edited by Norma Farnes. Many of
Spike Milligan's books are published in Penguins.

D1248021

I am the pen,
without me this paper
cannot live.

OPEN HEART UNIVERSITY

POEMS

Spike Milligan

illustrations by
Laura Milligan and Jack Hobbs and
Spike Milligan

PENGUIN BOOKS

Penguin Books Ltd, Harmondsworth,
Middlesex, England
Penguin Books, 625 Madison Avenue,
New York, New York 10022, U.S.A.
Penguin Books Australia Ltd, Ringwood,
Victoria, Australia
Penguin Books Canada Ltd, 2801 John Street,
Markham, Ontario, Canada L3R 1B4
Penguin Books (N.Z.) Ltd, 182–190 Wairau Road,
Auckland 10, New Zealand

First published by M. and J. Hobbs and Michael Joseph 1979
Published in Penguin Books 1980

Made and printed in Great Britain by
Butler and Tanner Ltd, Frome and London

This book is dedicated
to S.S. who gave me
heaven and hell

July 1978

Omen of emptiness

The clock has turned enough
        to reach a planet

Life is endless night
I hear wings beating in
        the dark of my room

A giant Raven is waiting –
        for me to fall asleep

Winter 1977

Laura Milligan

When I Suspected

There will be a time when it will end.
Be it parting
Be it death
So each passing minute with you
                          pendulumned with sadness.
So many times
I looked long into your face.
                     I could hear the clock ticking.

On a plane over Java
November 1977

Unfaithful She

Dedicated to S.S.

The sight of you
    rent the heaven in two
The gasp in your voice
    could do that too
That the sky would fall
    with a telephone call
And leave me standing in an empty hall.
So folly runs like wine
    but the empty glass is mine.
You leave no choice
    save the lasting taste of brine

Envoi

It was you,
    that poisoned the morning dew

Bayswater
November 1977

A Present for the Future

To Miss J.G.

Green earrings I bought her
       from Maori Shores.
When I returned,
       she had gone
and taken her ears with her.

Earrings made from Pacific Jade –
       you could see through them
Why didn't I see through her?

A-Have-It-Away-Day

To Miss J.G.

I asked a friend how I lost her.
'She met a man on a train
       and fell in love with him.'
Money is not all the British Railways are
       losing.

True Love, Until

Dedicated to S.S.

In bed she said 'I love you'
She said it to my face.
I remember as each silver word
Fell carefully in place.

Continental Envoi

In bed she said 'I love you'
To many another face.
And once again each silver word
Fell carefully in place.

January 1978

Feelings

There *must* be a wound!
No one can be this hurt
            and not bleed.

How could she injure me so?
            No marks
            No bruise

Worse!
People say 'My, you're looking well'
...... God help me!
            She's mummified me –
                        ALIVE!

                        Bayswater
                        December 1977

Feelings.

There must be a wound!
No one can be this hurt
          and not bleed.

How could she injure me so?
          No marks
          No bruise

Worse!
People say My, your looking well
..... God help me!
Shes mummyfied me —
               ALIVE!

Dec 77
Bayswalk

Welcome Home

Unaware of my crime
      they stood me in the dock.

I was sentenced to life . . . .
           without her.

Strange trial.
      No Judge.
      No Jury.

I wonder who my visitors will be.

Bayswater
December 1977

Revenge

To Miss J.G.

She once made beautiful Easter Eggs.
Down the years
       the clumsy broke theirs.
I kept mine safe.
Today, I broke it.
I used a dove's feather.
I'm not a vicious person.

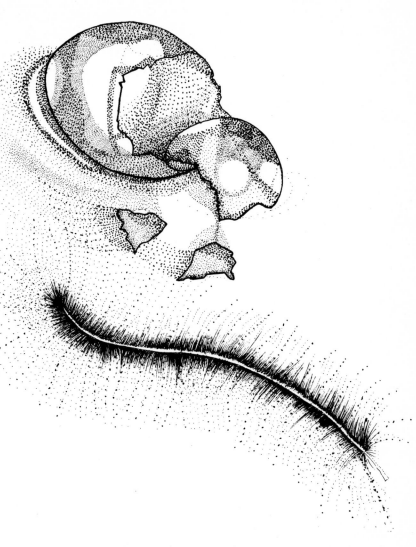

Laura Milligan

19

Goodbye S.S

Go away girl, go away
and let me pack my dreams
now where did S put those yesteryears
made up with broken seams
Where shall S sweep the pieces
my God they still look new
Theres a taxi waiting at the door
but theres only room for you

Food of Love.

Four years she ate my dinners
Four years she drank my wines
And all the while.
I was nourishing her
For some other crummy swines.

Bayswater
1477

Finale

The Queen stumbles
      the bones of heaven
      torque in winds of death.

Black Swans
      course the Styx.
Warriors burn your shields,
      sand the blood-folded fields.

Turrets catch the King's grief.
      White handed he paces the air
      with mindless fingers.

Fires sorrow the night
      in dead-finery she biers
Wax-ready for unknown journeys

Pass on black-blench waters. . . . .

Laura Milligan

The Light That Failed

To Shelagh

It's this darkness at noon –
I can hear the boat sailing
I thought I knew where the switch was
Everything was so bright,
The picture was nearly finished
Even the eyes seemed perfect
So what happened to the light?
It must have been an eclipse. . . . .
Mine. . . . .

1977

Laura Milligan

Eurolove

I cannot
   and I will not
   no, I cannot love you less
Like the flower to the butterfly
The corsage to the dress

She turns my love to dust
      my destination empty
         my beliefs scattered - Diaspora!

Who set this course. - and why?
Now my wings beat -
            without purpose
Yet they speed...........

Dedicated to S.S.

26

Laura Milligan

My Daughter of 5 – Jane

The midnight clock
    cuts hours into the dark

That picture of you
    stilled by sleep
    one dream ahead
    as children always are.

Little Jane
    you colour my tired mind
Opening gates in long forgotten
        child meadows
Where once I ran through summer grasses
    now, it grows for you.

Finchley
4 December 1969
1.40am

Easter 1916

The lights had gone out!
    The sun cannot set!
    The green heart is suppurating!
Heroes' souls are on the English rack
    and the harp's strings are muted.

In the fusillade
    a child is born in blood,
    his heritage will be glory.

Goodnight Padraic Pearse
    and your friends.

                February 1975

Spike Milligan

That we should meet
     so late
     so late.

Such preordemptioned
     bitter fate.

Sounding down
      an endless hall

The ticking clock
      against the wall

The closing hands
      upon its face

If we're to make love
      we'll have to race.

Maitland Bay, NSW
1976

Laura Mishigan

To Toni Savage and his
Old Wooden Printing Machine

When the great tree
Loomed from high-falling,
Her green head pitching down
Till the great body lay stillstraight,
Was she to be heard no more?
Men took her,
Piece by piece
And togethered her again,
In new bowen shape
    and from her dead body
Words came, and those printed sounds
Were stamped with loving care on
    the warp and binded weave
    of a paper made – from her sister.
Sober truth survives
Her breeze still blows
on the mind of men
and sinks such roots
As no tree, has ever sunk.

Laura Mishgan

Sun

Open ended orb
Timeless energen thing
Power beyond thought
Unharnessed might
Flaming! Hydrogen face of God
Did you have a population problem once
and solve it.?

Diane

When you unleash the dogs of you
Onto my greenacious field
I know they are hunting.

I have seen you before
     tree tall dream,
     hair like Dane Gelt

If you are true
     then hunt me down
     but make the kill quick
I cannot live long
     in your arrowed gaze

Messages on burned Restaurant quick paper
     carry cups of red assent
Let me spill them on your Oberon-blade corsage.

Hurry White Queen,
     My Sun is setting.

Abstract

Somewhere,
    deep in the miniscule microcosms
        of unknown time,
Lost in a space within space,
a Giant of nothingness.
No sight but vibra-senses can behold
        its roaring silence.
Fillings of lustrous unknown colours,
Such primeval cold that frost melts at its maw.
Endless ice-orchid sealed in weightless jade
        that sparks with Titanic fury
        melts rainbows that liquify
        into cups of feather like ore
        drunk by basalt black figures
        who claim to have seen God.

They say, if you look through the holes in Christ's
hands you can see,
Victoria Station, only its red.

In a plane over
the Red Sea
February 1977

39

To Doug Rouse-Woodcarver

Lonely man,
What's this strange tale?
Locked in some haunted
          man free forest
You welt a wooden virgin
That was taken by a swollen stream
And this new chiselled Mary
          quick with river child
Looks her Oaken eyes on a strange Bethlehem
She had never seen before.
Villagers, seeing her in her wild beauty
Took her, and locked her in the Post Office
So no trees would fall on her.
The lonely man carved her again
          so that her Jesus child
          would not be born in a Post Office.

Summer Dawn

My sleeping children are still flying dreams
      in their goose-down heads.
The lush of the river singing morning songs
Fish watch their ceilings turn sun-white.
The grey-green pike lances upstream
Kale, like mermaids' hair
      points the water's drift.
All is morning hush
      and bird beautiful.

If only,
    I didn't have flu.

Winchelsea
1961

42

Jack Hobbs

Rachmaninov's 3rd Piano Concerto

We are drinking cupped Sonatas like wine,
The red glow, the cut throat of Sunset.
Like a tungsten locked Icarus
I charge my mind with heaven fermented grape
that grow to Caesar's Royal Purple in my brain,
Trim my logic as I may
The tyrant Onos unbraids my thoughts
      like maidens' tresses at eve
I am wafting across mindless heavens
'Where am I,' I ask the Lotus maiden,
She says 'Singapore Air Lines –
      Economy Class'.

To A Victorian Doll in a shop window in Kensington Church Street - Priced £200

Beautiful, porcelain yester-doll,
    still wax fresh
Some little girl all ringlets
    and flounced lace
Loved you, cried on you, slept happy
    in your glass-eyed gaze.
Those long shed safe dreams
    have slipped their moorings.
That great red brick house
    spick-span polished proud
Now hard-boarded uni-rooms reeking
    curry, cabbage and cat's piss.
Polished doors lie Dulux deep,
    with red plastic handles.
So, dear home-less doll in the window
    waiting the right price
    they've turned you into a whore.

Laura Milligan

Open Heart University

Dedicated to BBC-TV Open University

We've come a long way
      said the Cigarette Scientist
as he destroyed a live rabbit
      to show the students how it worked.

He took its heart out
      plugged it into an electric pump
      that kept it beating for nearly two hours.

I know rabbits who can keep their hearts
      beating for nearly seven years

And look at the electricity they save.

London
March 1977

Laura Milligan

I thought I saw Jesus
on a tram.
I said 'Are you Jesus?'
He said 'Yes I am'.

I thought I saw Jesus
    on a Tram.
I said 'Are you Jesus'
He said "Yes I am'.

M.1. Way of Life

Bloody, Battered, Tattered Thing
Which is body
Which is wing
What kind of bird
It's hard to say
As you lay squashed
On a motor way
But the marks in your blood
Are sharp and clear
A Dunlop 'safety' tyre
Has just been here.

Laura Milligan

I had walked out of the dead winter.
I could see a Spring child laughing through
                              the window.
Unseen fruit pulses in the arms of
                              winter trees
Young to be-bees think of honey
soon –
One less bee
One less Spring
One more Winter.

Los Angeles
June 1975

Child Songs

There is a song in man
There is a song in woman
And that is the child's song
When that song comes
There will be no words
Do not ask where they are
Just listen to the song
Listen to it –
Learn it –
It is the greatest song of all.

London
12 April 1973
0200 hours

Strange lovers may caress you
but once, long ago
you were mine for ever,
So should I reach into that past
and touch you with invisible fingers
dont move away.

Laura Milligan

Letters

I was thinking of letters,
We all have a lot in our life
A few good – a few sad
But mostly run of the mill –
I suppose that's my fault
For writing to run of the mill people.
I've never had a letter
I *really* wanted
It might come one day
But then, it will be just too late,
And that's when I don't want it.

Timeless time and endless days
The world around us standing still
Like photographs
Of deserted shafts
Of statues left on distant hills
Two ghostly stands
In a giant's hands
We would walk together,
You and I
And the only word
From the mocking bird
Was love.

The sheer delight
Of endless light
What used to be
A barren tree
Was growing flowers overnight
And scenting it with ecstasy
A cup of coffee from your hand
Becomes the gold of Samarkand.

The swallows came and flew away
As the early dust of Autumn leaves
Were settling slow
On the afterglow
On a lasting love that could not die
When suddenly
On a tideless sea
How the glass that held us both together
Shattered and the whole damned thing went wrong.

A thousand nights
A thousand days
Are bitter pills
Time can't erase
The child we grew
Within us two
Will never know our golden days
He'll never walk
or laugh or run
Into a field
A setting sun . . . .

Laura Milligan

Catford 1933

The light creaks
    and escalates to rusty dawn
The iron stove ignites the freezing room.
Last night's dinner cast off
    popples in the embers.
My mother lives in a steaming sink.
Boiled haddock condenses on my plate
    Its body cries for the sea.
My father is shouldering his braces like a rifle,
    and brushes the crumbling surface of his suit.
The *Daily Herald* lays jaundiced on the table.
'Jimmy Maxton speaks in Hyde Park',
My father places his unemployment cards
    in his wallet – there's plenty of room for them.
In greaseproof paper, my mother wraps my
        banana sandwiches.
It's 5.40. Ten minutes to catch that
    last workman train.
Who is the last workman? Is it me? I might be famous.
My father and I walk out and are eaten by
    yellow freezing fog.
Somewhere, the Prince of Wales
    and Mrs Simpson are having morning tea in bed.
God Save the King.
But God help the rest of us.

Trust

Painful though it was,
    I cut my last winter rose for her.

She turned it inside out
    to see who the manufacturer was.

January 1978

I went to the Jazz Club.
Young over-amplified men played Saxophones
They played very fast –
Perhaps they had a bus to catch?
The drummer played very loud,
Was he deaf?
They were very accomplished musicians
The music didn't touch me
I couldn't hear the tune for the noise.
'It's not in here' said an old man.
He took me to an old house,
Dust lay thick on forgotten chairs.
In the corner was an embalmed piano
The old man raised the lid and pointed.
'It's in there' he said.

London
December 1974

'A' Levels

Those energy wrought children
    their limbs loaded into school desks.
In the shadows they are fed
        Algebra – Science – Syntax.

Outside, the ignorant
    are laughing and playing
    in the Sun.

Bayswater
January 1978

America I Love You

The fur bearing lady
       said to the Jeweller
'Can you fashion a rose of
       gold or silver?'
'Yes' said he
'Which is cheaper?' said she
'A real one' said he
'Real' said the lady, 'that's
       for the poor people.'

Los Angeles
1977.

India! India!

As a boy
I watched India through fresh Empirical eyes.
Inside my young khaki head
I grew not knowing any other world.
My father was a great warrior
My mother was beautiful
                and never washed dishes,
                other people did that,
I was only 4, I remember
                they cleaned my shoes,
                made my bed.
'Ither ow'
'Kom Kurrow'
Yet, in time I found them gentler
                than the khaki people
They smiled in their poverty
After dark, when the khaki people
                were drunk in the mess
I could hear Minnima and
                her family praying in their godown.
In the bazaar the khaki men
                are brawling
No wonder they asked us to leave.

If a bird in a cage
    puts all heaven in a Rage.
How feels heaven when
    dies the billioneth battery hen

Floating Dandelion Seed

Wonderful wandering sky child
  seeking one piece of
    fertile soil

Alas, you don't find that
  in a railway station buffet
    so, you die.

But then, given time, a railway station
  buffet would kill us all.

My Love is Like a . . . .

If I gave her red roses
    would she?
If I gave her white roses
    in a bowl of wine
      would she?
I gave her green carnations
    made from dollar bills
      – and she did.

It was black.
It walked up a tree.
In the nest: a day old sparrow.
The black creature tore it apart.
That night
The black creature lay by the fire.
A lady stroked it.
"Nice pussy" she said.

I walked along some forgotten shore.
Coming the other way
          a smiling boy.
It was me.
'Who are you old man?' he said
I dare not tell him all I could say was
'Go back!'

Madrid
14 September 1973